35 Affordable Waterfront Retirement Towns

Best U.S. Towns for an Affordable Retirement Along a Lake, River or Seacoast

Written and Edited by Kris Kelley

Published by

Webwerxx, Inc.

17101 E. Baltic Dr., Aurora, Colorado   80013

Notes

Cost of living numbers include housing, medical, transportation, food, utilities and taxes. This publication contains information from several sources. Numerous efforts have been made to verify the accuracy of the information in this book, but some information may have changed since publication. This especially applies to the median home price, median rent price and cost of living number in small towns as these are particularly sensitive to market changes. As a result, Webwerxx, Inc. cannot guarantee the accuracy of the content contained within this publication.

ISBN-13:
978-1537495613

Table of Contents

Introduction

Living near the water is a lifelong dream for many people. So when retirement time arrives, moving to a lakeside town or a seaside community is a natural inclination. The trick is to find a town that is reasonably priced.

Here we have 35 towns that sit next to a lake, have a lake within their boundaries or are along a river or seacoast. They have a cost of living that meets the national average or is below the national average. They also have a crime rate that is equal to or below the national rate.

No place is perfect, however, so we point out each town's potential drawbacks. We also look at population, climate, home prices, percentage of residents age 45 or better, medical facilities, public transportation, crime rates, political leanings and more.

And when it comes to political leanings, it is worth noting that many of the towns in this book are in the South where lakes are plentiful. Small Southern towns tend to be conservative.

Cedar Bluff, Alabama

Cedar Bluff sits directly on the shore of pretty Weiss Lake in the quiet countryside of northeastern Alabama. Started as a roadway crossing and close to two Civil War sites, the town has been growing, increasing its population by 15% within the last decade.

The lake is fed by three rivers and covers more than 30,000 acres. Boating and waterskiing are popular, but the lake is particularly known for its crappie and bass fishing.

Wooded neighborhoods meander and have modest ranch ramblers, nicer plantation styles and some condominiums. Lakefront homes have boat docks and piers.

Most commercial buildings are low slung, and banks, churches, shopping centers and strip malls with auto parts stores, pawn shops, convenience stores, fishing supply stores and similar are located here and there.

Restaurants are mostly sub shops, barbeque joints, diners and family-style establishments. There are a couple of lakefront parks with boat ramps. Shopping is limited to some local retailers, Kmart and Walmart.

Population: 1,900 (city proper)

Percentage of Population Age 45 or Better: 42%

Cost of Living: 12% below the national average

Median Home Price: $135,000

Median Monthly Rent: $1,195

Climate: Summer temperatures are in the 80s and 90s, and winter temperatures are in the 30s and 40s. On average, the area receives 55 inches of rain and 2 inches of snow each year.

At Least One Hospital Accepts Medicare Patients? No, but Cherokee Medical Center is 5 miles away in Centre and accepts Medicare patients.

At Least One Hospital Accredited by Joint Commission? No, but Cherokee Medical Center is 5 miles away in Centre and is accredited.

Public Transit: No

Crime Rate: Below the national average

Public Library: No

Political Leanings: Very, very conservative

Is Alabama Considered Tax Friendly for Retirement? Yes

Drawbacks: The tornado risk is 225% greater than the national average, and the poverty rate is above the national average.

Notes: The air quality is outstanding. Cedar Bluff is a simple place but one people seem to enjoy. Atlanta is two hours to the southeast.

Guntersville, Alabama

In the lush hills of northeastern Alabama, sleepy but growing Guntersville is tucked along a stretch of Lake Guntersville's 900 miles of shoreline and is an appealing small town in a beautiful setting. The 69,000-acre lake is the center of life here and is particularly popular with bass fishermen.

The town is nearly surrounded by water, and the city harbor has some new docks. In addition to bass fishing, residents enjoy canoeing, water skiing and bird watching.

The cute, authentic downtown, which is non-touristy, has awning-draped, one story and two story red and blond brick buildings that house clothiers, banks, bookstores and more. Residents enjoy a Civil War museum, a Native American museum and a thriving parks and recreation department with a good menu of athletic programs for adults.

The Whole Backstage, which is more than forty years old, presents six to seven full scale theater productions each season. An arts council promotes concerts, art festivals and juried competitions.

Good, locally owned restaurants are in good supply and serve everything from fried catfish to hush puppies. Chain eateries include Subway, McDonald's and others.

Homes include hillside cabins, bungalows, brick ranch ramblers and waterfront properties with a boat house. Most residences sit on wooded lots.

Lake Guntersville State Park is along the Tennessee River is just northeast of town and has a beach complex, an 18-hole golf course, hiking trails and a campground.

Population: 8,300 (city proper)

Percentage of Population Age 45 or Better: 45%

Cost of Living: 10% below the national average

Median Home Price: $140,000

Median Monthly Rent: $795

Climate: Summer temperatures are in the 80s and 90s, and winter temperatures are in the 30s, 40s, and 50s.   On average, the area receives 52 inches of rain per year.

At Least One Hospital Accepts Medicare Patients? Yes

At Least One Hospital Accredited by Joint Commission? Yes

Public Transit: Yes, a call ahead van service

Crime Rate: Meets the national average

Public Library: Yes

Political Leanings: Very conservative

Is Alabama Considered Tax Friendly for Retirement? Yes

Drawbacks: The tornado risk is 290% higher than the national average.

Notes: Locals also say that a bit of a "good ole boy" network exists, particularly in some political circles. Guntersville has grown by 4% within the last decade.

Pell City, Alabama

On the shores of 17,000 Logan Martin Lake in northeastern Alabama, easygoing Pell City is St. Clair County's largest and fastest growing community. It is just half an hour to the east of Birmingham, the state's largest city (population 215,000).

The lake is the main draw here, and Lakeside Park has walking fishing piers, a swim area and direct access to the water. Logan Martin has eight marinas and 275 miles of shoreline. The annual boat show and Lakefest are popular events. Fishing tournaments happen year-round.

The downtown is dotted with specialty shops and loft apartments, and the Artscape Gallery and Council for the Arts hold an annual art festival. The Pell City Center houses a community theater and a sports arena. The Hometown Block Party, featuring music and home-style food, draws large crowds.

The Toughman Alabama Triathlon brings out local athletes, and two golf courses attract players of all ages. Other recreation facilities include an outdoor sports complex and an indoor cardio center.

Strip malls along U.S. 231 have banks, fast food places, discount stores and the like.

Neighborhoods are well kept, and many homes are on large lots. Architectural styles include brick Colonial, ranch rambler, plantation and others.

Population: 13,000 (city proper)

Percentage of Population Age 45 or Better: 41%

Cost of Living: 13% below the national average

Median Home Price: $135,000

Median Monthly Rent: $1,185

Climate: Summer temperatures are in the 80s and 90s, and winter temperatures are in the 30s and 40s. On average, the area receives 49 inches of rain each year.

At Least One Hospital Accepts Medicare Patients? Yes

At Least One Hospital Accredited by Joint Commission?
No, but Citizens Baptist Medical Center is 15 miles away
in Talladega and is accredited.

Public Transit: No

Crime Rate: Meets the national average

Public Library: Yes

Political Leanings: Very, very conservative

Is Alabama Considered Tax Friendly for Retirement? Yes

Drawbacks: The tornado risk is 260% greater than the
national average.

Notes: The air quality is outstanding. Pell City grown by
30% within the last decade.

Lake Havasu, Arizona

Lake Havasu City, Arizona is located along the Arizona -
California border and sits on the eastern shore of Lake
Havasu, a large, shimmering reservoir that was created by
the construction of Parker Dam in the 1930s. Originally
created as a planned community for Army Air Corps
personnel during World War II, Lake Havasu City was later
purchased by chainsaw industry mogul Robert McCulloch
in 1963.

Since those early days, the city has evolved into a popular
tourist destination, attracting 3.5 million visitors a year
(including some college Spring Break revelers). Retirees,

many from California, have discovered the city, too, and it has flourished, growing by 25% in the last 10 years

Residents enjoy a good menu of restaurants serving everything from Chinese to Italian cuisine. The Shops at Lake Havasu City has national retailers, including J.C. Penney, Walmart and Dillard's.

The city has a pretty desert landscape with mountains nearby, and it is often hailed as one of North America's preeminent water sports hubs. Lake Havasu is an ideal environment for jet skiing, wind surfing, wakeboarding, sailing and bass fishing. Boat rentals are always available if the need arises.

For a more rustic excursion, Lake Havasu State Park boasts a full tapestry of beautiful scenery from Windsor Beach to Cattail Cove with rolling hills in between. Hiking, camping and fishing are among the activities enjoyed in this historic state park.

Population: 53,000 (city proper)

Percentage of Population Age 45 or Better: 53%

Cost of Living: Meets the national average

Median Home Price: $180,000

Median Monthly Rent: $1,290

Climate: Summer high temperatures are in the 90s and low-100s, and winters are mild with temperatures in 40s, 50s, 60s and 70s. On average, the area receives 3 inches of rain per year.

At Least One Hospital Accepts Medicare Patients? Yes

At Least One Hospital Accredited by Joint Commission?
Yes

Public Transit: Yes

Crime Rate: Below the national average

Public Library: Yes

Political Leanings: Very conservative

Is Arizona Considered Tax Friendly for Retirement? Yes

Drawbacks: Flash floods have occurred in the past.

Notes: Lake Havasu is the home of the original London
Bridge, which Robert McCulloch purchased from the city
of London, England in 1967. Today, the bridge is
Arizona's second most popular tourist attraction. The
Grand Canyon is the most popular.

Conway, Arkansas

Only 35 minutes from Little Rock in central Arkansas,
suburban Conway is one of state's largest cities and
receives good reviews.   It has been growing very fast and
has three colleges within its boundaries.   The largest of
these is the University of Central Arkansas with 14,500
students.

Lake Conway, just south of the city, is a fishermen's dream.
It boasts 6,700 acres brimming with bass, bream and
bowfin.   Boaters love the lake, too. Beaverfork Lake, one
of Conway's many parks, has a lush shoreline and a fishing
dock.

Residents enjoy a driving range as well as country clubs with golf courses. The city's most popular festival is Toad Suck Daze, three days of live music, arts, and toad races that benefit local scholarship funds.

The University hosts the nationally known Arkansas Shakespeare Theatre. The Conway Symphony Orchestra plays in the university's Reynolds Performance Hall.

The downtown has a mid-20th century feeling with two story brick buildings that house a mix of retailers, a farmers' market and an outdoor cinema. The city's new expo center hosts the Arkansas Outdoors Expo and has a steak cook-off and a duck calling contest.

Residences, whether in modest neighborhoods or custom home enclaves, are mostly ranch ramblers and split levels made from brick.

Population: 65,000 (city proper)

Percentage of Population Age 45 or Better: 25%

Cost of Living: 10% below the national average

Median Home Price: $140,000

Median Monthly Rent: $995

Climate: Conway has a humid subtropical climate. Summer temperatures are in the 80s and 90s, and winter temperatures are in the 30s, 40s and 50s. The area receives 50 inches of rain and a dusting of snow each year, on average.

At Least One Hospital Accepts Medicare Patients? Yes

At Least One Hospital Accredited by the Joint Commission?   Yes

Public Transit: Yes

Crime Rate: Meets the national average

Public Library: Yes

Political Leanings: Very conservative

Is Arkansas Considered Tax Friendly for Retirement?   Yes

Drawbacks: The tornado risk is 285% above the national average.

Notes: Thirty-six percent of Conway residents have a bachelor's degree or higher.

Fairfield Bay, Arkansas

Tucked on the shores of pretty 40,000-acre Greers Ferry Lake in the Ozark Mountains of rural north central Arkansas, Fairfield Bay was founded in the mid-1960s as a resort and retirement community. Vacationers still come by the thousands each year, primarily to stay and play at the Wyndham Resort at Fairfield Bay.

Swimming, cliff diving and scuba diving are some of the recreation options available at Greers Ferry Lake. Plenty of walleye, bass and crappie keep fishermen happy. The full-service marina includes a campground, boat rentals and a ships' store. A water trolley takes passengers to the Sugar Loaf Mountain Nature Trail.   Residents also enjoy two golf courses, three swimming pools and fitness centers.

Fairfield Bay and its neighborhoods are thickly wooded and have a distinctly mountain ambiance. Modest homes sit close together just off of country roads while expensive residences are set back in the woods and have acreage. Lakefront homes have piers and boat docks.

There is no classic town core, but banks, diners, gas stations and convenience stores are scattered here and there. Social activities include outdoor movies, concerts, Storyfest, the American Legion Golf Classic and Surf the Bay Watersport Festival. An HOA fee allows residents access to all of the community's amenities.

Although Fairfield Bay is off the beaten path, roads throughout the community are paved and in generally good shape. Residents are just a short distance from shopping in Conway, entertainment in Branson and big city life in Little Rock.

Population: 2,400 (city proper)

Percentage of Population Age 45 or Better: 77%

Cost of Living: 18% below the national average

Median Home Price: $105,000

Median Monthly Rent: $775

Climate: Fairfield Bay has a humid, four-season climate. Summer temperatures are in the 80s and 90s. Winters are mild, with temperatures in the 30s, 40s and 50s. On average, the area receives 50 inches of rain per year.

At Least One Hospital Accepts Medicare Patients? No, but Ozark Health in Clinton, 10 miles away, accepts Medicare patients.

At Least One Hospital Accredited by Joint Commission?
No, but Baptist Health in Heber Springs, 10 miles away, is accredited.

Public Transit: No

Crime Rate: Well below the national average

Public Library: Yes

Political Leanings: Very conservative

Is Arkansas Considered Tax Friendly for Retirement?
Yes

Drawbacks: The town is losing population, about 2% within the last decade, and the tornado risk is 145% higher than the national average.

Notes: Homeowners have to pay HOA fees. These allow access to the amenities.

Alva, Florida

Easygoing Alva straddles the Caloosahatchee River at the western edge of the Okeechobee Waterway in southwestern Florida. Less than an hour from Fort Myers and Cape Coral, it stretches over 18 square miles and continues to fight to retain its rural character in the face of encroaching development from the west.

Grazing cattle, citrus groves and large oak trees with hanging moss dot the local landscape, evoking a sense of Old Florida. The first bridge over the Caloosahatchee was built in Alva in 1903, and its boat launch is still in use today.

The town is home to Eden Winery, one of the southernmost vineyards in the U.S., and the active garden club curates the local museum and sponsors talks by master gardeners.

Palm Beach Boulevard on the southern edge of town has convenience stores, gas stations and fast food places, but most shopping takes place in Ft. Myers, twenty miles to the west, or in Lehigh Acres, eight miles to the south.

Alva is bracketed by three preserves, and Hickey Creek has hiking trails, a kayak landing, and a fishing deck. The Caloosahatchee Regional Park has campgrounds, guided walks and biking trails.

Some Alva neighborhoods have country lots, while others have small home sites and feel more suburban. A few areas, including the River Hall Golf and Country Club, are peppered with ponds.

Housing stock includes Mediterranean styles, ranch ramblers, manufactured homes and more. Cascades at River Hall is a 55+ single family home community.

Population: 2,500 (city proper)

Percentage of Population Age 45 or Better: 55%

Cost of Living: Meets the national average

Median Home Price: $190,000

Median Monthly Rent: $1,400

Climate: Summers are warm with highs in the upper 80s and low 90s. Winters have temperatures in the 50s, 60s and 70s. On average, the area receives 50 inches of rain per year.

At Least One Hospital Accepts Medicare Patients? No, but Lehigh Regional Medical Center, just eight miles away, accepts Medicare patients.

At Least One Hospital Accredited by Joint Commission? No, but Lehigh Regional Medical Center, just eight miles away, is accredited by the Joint Commission.

Public Transit: No

Crime Rate: Well below the national average

Public Library: No

Political Leanings: Conservative

Is Florida Considered Tax Friendly for Retirement? Yes

Drawbacks: Lehigh Regional Medical Center does not receive good patient reviews. Ft. Myers has several hospitals, but they are 10 to 20 miles away.

Notes: Alva has grown by 7% within the last ten years.

Beverly Beach, Florida

This tiny, tightly knit Flagler County town is only 1.3 miles long and sits on a barrier island between the Matanzas River and the Atlantic Ocean on Florida's northeastern coast. Scenic Highway A1A runs through it.

Primarily residential with a beautiful beach, Beverly Beach has older seaside homes, some condominiums and Surfside Estates, a large, compact mobile home park for people age 55 or better. Sunset Inlet is a new housing development with conch style homes and boat docks.

Camptown RV Resort sits between A1A and the ocean. It has a general store, but most shopping and commercial services are in Flagler Beach or Palm Coast, the town's next door neighbors.

Herschel King Park has a riverside boat ramp and canoe launch. Fishing is permitted on the beach and on the riverside seawall.

Nearby attractions include the Graham Swamp Conservation Area and the Washington Oaks State Park. The centerpiece of Washington Oaks is a formal garden, but there are also short trails for hiking and biking.

Population: 435 (city proper)

Percentage of Population Age 45 or Better: 80%

Cost of Living: 6% below national average

Median Home Price: $140,000

Median Rent: $780 per month

Climate: Summer temperatures are in the 80s and 90s, and winter temperatures are in the 50s, 60s and 70s. On average, Beverly Beach receives 50 inches of rain per year.

At Least One Hospital Accepts Medicare Patients? No, but Florida Hospital Flagler, four miles away in Palm Coast, accepts Medicare patients.

At Least One Hospital Accredited by Joint Commission? No, but Florida Hospital Flagler, four miles away in Palm Coast, is accredited.

Public Transit: Flagler County Public Transportation has an on demand van system that runs through the County.

Crime Rate: Well below the national average

Public Library: No

Political Leanings: Conservative

Is Florida Considered Tax Friendly for Retirement? Yes

Drawbacks: The town is completely exposed if a hurricane should strike.

Notes: The RV resort is popular with "snowbirds." Even though Beverly Beach is tiny, it has a mayor, commissioners and a town hall. Flagler Beach's senior center, which is just down the road, provides hot lunches, computer help and has a lending library.

The town has lost 10% of its population in the last 10 years, but with people now moving into Sunset Inlet, the population is increasing again. Taxes related to Sunset Inlet are also helping increase town revenues.

Deerfield Beach, Florida

Deerfield Beach is situated along the congested southeastern Florida coast and started out as an agricultural community. It was named Deerfield for the deer grazing in the fields and remained a farming hub until the 1940s when it changed its name to Deerfield Beach in an effort to attract tourists.

Today, the town does attract sun worshippers but not in the numbers seen by some of its neighbors. Clean and often uncrowded, the one mile long beach has been renovated and is award winning. It has a 920 foot long fishing pier and a nicely manicured, palm lined buffer between it and a boardwalk with mom and pop shops and restaurants. Hotels and condominiums are across the street from the boardwalk.

The city has nineteen parks, including Quiet Waters Park, which has water skiing, fishing, mountain bike trails and camping spots. Deerfield Park is a large nature preserve, and the Deerfield Arboretum receives rave reviews.

Downtown is busy with a mix of tall glass office buildings, chain restaurants, banks, parking garages and the like. The Country Music Festival and the National Night Out are just two of many community events.

Restaurants are in good supply and include everything from BBQ joints to Italian bistros. Shopping malls include Hillsboro Square, which has nearly fifty retailers.

Housing stock includes modest ranch ramblers, sleek Mediterranean style homes, condominiums and more.

Population: 75,000 (city proper)

Percentage of Population Age 45 or Better: 50%

Cost of Living: 6% below the national average

Median Home Price: $127,000

Median Rent: $1,250 per month

Climate: This area has a tropical monsoon climate. The area receives 58 inches of rain per year, on average.

At Least One Hospital Accepts Medicare Patients?   No, but Boca Raton Regional Hospital and North Broward Medical Center are within five miles and accept Medicare patients.

At Least One Hospital is Accredited by Joint Commission? No, but Boca Raton Regional Hospital and North Broward Medical Center are within five miles and are accredited.

Public Transit: Yes, provided by Broward County Transit. A para-transit service is also available.

Crime Rate: Meets the national average

Public Library: Yes

Political Leanings: Liberal

Is Florida Considered Tax Friendly for Retirement? Yes

Drawbacks: Hurricanes are always a possibility.

Notes: Deerfield Beach is racially diverse, home to Brazilians, Haitians, Cubans and other groups.   U.S. Route 1 runs through the city.

Gulfport, Florida

Sitting on the shores of the Boca Ciega Bay, this casual west central Florida town started out in the late-19th century and had three names before settling on Gulfport. It is just east of St. Petersburg and is known for its Old Florida waterfront district and artsy, bohemian vibe.

Neighborhoods are laid out along grids. Inland homes are mostly modest concrete block styles while canal-front homes are generally gorgeous and have a boat slip. Bayfront condominium buildings are here, too.

Beach Boulevard, which ends at the water, is lined with one story buildings that house colorful restaurants, quirky shops and fun bookstores. Shore Boulevard parallels the narrow beach and is peppered with parking areas, apartments, green spaces, modest homes and palm trees.

The marina has a seawall, wet slips and fueling stations, and Williams Pier is popular with anglers and bird watchers. Tuesday is Fresh Market day, and art walks happen on the first Friday and third Saturday of each month.

The pastel green Gulfport Casino Ballroom sits next to the water and offers anything from Argentine tango to Salsa five nights per week. Gulfport operates a theater and a senior center, and the local library has a reading garden and supports a writing group.

Clam Bayou Nature Park boasts boardwalks, trails, observation decks, docks, and a kayak launch. Chase Park is the home of the historical society's museum, and Wood Ibis Park has a lake and a butterfly park.

Population: 12,500 (city proper)

Percentage of Population Age 45 or Better: 54%

Cost of Living: 8% below the national average

Median Home Price: $160,000

Median Monthly Rent: $1,300

Climate: This area has a humid subtropical climate, meaning two seasons a year. Summer and early fall are hot and humid. Late fall and winter are less humid and cooler. On average, the area receives 48 inches of rain per year.

At Least One Hospital Accepts Medicare Patients? No, but St. Petersburg has several hospitals that accept Medicare patients.

At Least One Hospital Accredited by Joint Commission? No, but St. Petersburg has several accredited hospitals.

Public Transit: Yes

Crime Rate: Meets the national average

Public Library: Yes

Political Leanings: Liberal

Is Florida Considered Tax Friendly for Retirement? Yes

Drawbacks: Gulfport is losing population, about 5% in the last decade.

Notes: Some neighborhoods have seen better days.

Lady Lake, Florida

This northernmost Lake County town is a midpoint between Florida's two coasts and about an hour north west of Orlando. It is a pleasant, safe place and has part of the large, master-planned 55+ development The Villages within its borders. The rest of The Villages abuts Lady Lake to the west.

The County has 500 lakes, and many of them, including Lake Sunshine and Lake Ella, are scattered about town or just outside of town limits. Lake Griffin State Park is less than ten minutes away and has dockside fishing, a boat ramp and boat rentals. The nearby Ocala National Forest permits hiking, horseback riding, and canoeing.

Eight public golf courses are in or near Lady Lake, and the town's Heritage Park has a gazebo and one of Florida's oldest oaks. There is also a dog park and a Tuesday farmers' market.

Housing not within The Villages includes manufactured homes, concrete block dwellings, wood frame ranch ramblers, modest Mediterranean styles and others.

The Villages Lifelong Learning College has classes for Village and non-Village residents. Events in town include the Blue Parrot Craft Show and a Taste of Lady Lake.

Major retailers include Bealls, Target, Kohl's and more. Restaurants are mostly family-style chains. The Villages has three town centers, movie theaters, shopping, dining and more open to both residents and non-residents.

Population: 14,000 (city proper)

Percentage of Population Age 45 or Better: 80%

Cost of Living: Meets the national average

Median Home Price: $175,000

Median Monthly Rent: $1,395

Climate: Summer temperatures are in the 80s and 90s, and winter temperatures are in the 50s and 60s. On average, the area receives 48 inches of rain per year.

At Least One Hospital Accepts Medicare Patients? No, but The Villages Regional Hospital, two miles away, accepts Medicare patients.

At Least One Hospital Accredited by Joint Commission? No, but The Villages Regional Hospital, two miles away, is accredited.

Public Transit: Yes

Crime Rate: Below the national average

Public Library Yes

Political Leanings: Conservative

Is Florida Considered Tax Friendly for Retirement? Yes

Drawbacks: The tornado risk is 115% greater than the national average.

Notes: Lady Lake has grown by nearly 20% within the last ten years.

Laguna Beach, Florida

Low key Laguna Beach is an elongated, unincorporated community on the Florida Panhandle coast, about two miles west of Panama City Beach. On one side of town is the Gulf of Mexico and on the other side is beautiful Conservation Park, a 3,000-acre wetland area with walking trails and a few alligators.

Essentially the quieter side of Panama City Beach, Laguna Beach has a long, wide stretch of sugar white sand tucked against emerald waters. The town is mostly residential, and its beach is lined by large homes, vacation rentals, motels and short condominiums.

Neighborhoods are modest with an unfinished feeling. Stubby palm trees line narrow streets without sidewalks, and architectural styles include bungalows and conch styles.

Beach access points pepper Front Beach Road, which is the main drag that runs along the western edge of town. Busy Panama City Beach Parkway runs along the eastern edge.

Nearly all services, shopping venues and amenities are in Panama City Beach.

Population: 3,200 (city proper)

Percentage of Population Age 45 or Better: 52%

Cost of Living: Meets the national average

Median Home Price: $175,000

Median Monthly Rent: $1,250

Climate: Summer temperatures are in the 80s and 90s, and winter temperatures are in the 50s, 60s and 70. On average, the area receives 65 inches of rain per year.

At Least One Hospital Accepts Medicare Patients? No, but Gulf Coast Medical Center, 15 miles away in Panama City, accepts Medicare patients.

At Least One Hospital Accredited by Joint Commission? No, but Gulf Coast Medical Center, 15 miles away in Panama City, is accredited.

Public Transit: A bus runs along Front Beach Road and connects to Panama City Beach.

Crime Rate: Below the national average

Public Library: No

Political Leanings: Very, very conservative

Is Florida Considered Tax Friendly for Retirement? Yes

Drawbacks: Hurricanes are always a possibility, and Laguna Beach is completely exposed.

Notes: None

Land O' Lakes, Florida

Named for the large number of lakes within its borders, pretty, residential Land O' Lakes is at the northern edge of the Tampa metropolitan area.   New Port Richey is about 30 miles to the west and has a beach park.

Land O' Lakes has experienced rapid growth in the past 20 years, absorbing smaller towns and building neighborhoods at a quick pace.   Attractive, newer developments include Wellington Estates and Lake Padgett Estates.   Many neighborhoods sit along one of the lakes, and boat docks are common.

The County's recreation complex includes a pool, a fishing pier and a dog park. The Conner Preserve has a model airplane field and permits biking, while Cypress Creek Preserve allows fishing and hiking. Starkey Wilderness Park has horseback trails and cabins.   The Suncoast Trail, part of Florida's lush greenway system, winds through the area.

Shopping venues include strip malls and stand-alone retailers, many along busy Land O Lakes Boulevard. The Shops at Wireglass, an open air "lifestyle center" is about fifteen minutes away in Wesley Chapel. It has a Macy's, a J.C. Penney, a Barnes and Noble, a Williams-Sonoma and many others.

This area is known for its nudist resorts, and at least one of these is in Land O' Lakes. Two more are four miles to the south in Lutz.

Population: 33,000 (city proper)

Percentage of Population Age 45 or Better: 36%

Cost of Living: Meets the national average

Median Home Price: $185,000

Median Monthly Rent: $1,450

Climate: This area has a humid subtropical climate. Summer temperatures are in the 80s and 90s, and winter temperatures are in the 50s, 60s and 70s. On average, the area receives 48 inches of rain per year.

At Least One Hospital Accepts Medicare Patients? No, but Tampa has hospitals that accept Medicare patients.

At Least One Hospital Accredited by Joint Commission? No, but Tampa has accredited hospitals.

Public Transit: No

Crime Rate: Well below the national average

Public Library: Yes, and it has afternoon movies, book clubs, computer classes and a seniors' group with workshops, coffee get-togethers and recreational activities.

Political Leanings: Conservative

Is Florida Considered Tax Friendly for Retirement? Yes

Notes: Land O' Lakes has grown by nearly 55% in the last decade. The median household income is well above the national median.

Drawbacks: The tornado risk is 122% higher than the national average.

Mary Esther, Florida

About 35 miles east of Pensacola, this western Panhandle coastal town is wedged between Fort Walton Beach, Santa Rosa Sound and the U. S. Air Force's Hurlburt Field. It is a generally quiet, suburban place, home to many military personnel and their families.

Neighborhoods are neatly laid out, tidy and have an abundance of brick ranch ramblers. More elaborate single family homes and condos are along the water, but the majority of residences are inland.

Most shopping occurs at the Santa Rosa Mall, not a fancy place but with enough small stores and national retailers to meet basic needs.

The town manages its own community garden, a fertile piece of ground with gardeners who employ sustainable practices such composting and rain water collection. Mary

Esther also maintains 10 public parks, the largest of which is Oak Tree Nature Park.

The town's Pier Park includes a boat ramp and fishing facilities. Santa Rosa Island, across the sound from Mary Esther, is part of the Gulf Islands National Seashore and is open for swimming, bicycling, snorkeling, and beach combing. Its Pirate Cove is an excellent place to catch red fish and spotted sea trout.

Population: 4,000 (city proper)

Percentage of Population Age 45 or Better: 39%

Cost of Living: Meets the national average

Median Home Price: $185,000

Median Monthly Rent: $1,250

Climate: This area has a humid subtropical climate, meaning two seasons per year, one hot and humid and one less hot and less humid. On average, the area receives 65 inches of rain per year.

At Least One Hospital Accepts Medicare Patients? No, but Fort Walton Beach Medical Center, 3 miles away, accepts Medicare patients.

At Least One Hospital Accredited by Joint Commission? No, but Fort Walton Beach Medical Center, 3 miles away, is accredited.

Public Transit: Yes

Crime Rate: Below the national average

Public Library: The Mary Esther Public Library has book discussion groups and movie matinees.

Political Leanings: Very conservative

Is Florida Considered Tax Friendly for Retirement?   Yes

Drawbacks: Hurricanes and tropical storms are always a possibility.

Notes: Mary Esther sits along U.S. Route 98, a primary east-west highway, and the road can become very congested during summer tourist season.   This is bear country, and the city works with residents to help them coexist with the growing bear population.   The air quality is outstanding, and the town has grown by 3% within the last decade.

Mount Dora, Florida

Nestled in gentle hills along the edges of Lake Dora in central Florida, sleepy Mount Dora came into being in 1874 and may be one of Florida's prettiest towns, reminiscent of a quaint New England village. In fact, "Little New England" is its nickname.

Mount Dora is one of three lush, historic towns that make up an area known as the "Golden Triangle."   It is a popular place with retirees and boasts moss-draped hardwoods, waterfront parks and tidy streets that wind around nine shimmering lakes.

Leafy neighborhoods with manicured gardens have an eclectic mix of housing, from traditional Florida crackers and Victorian painted ladies to newer construction and gated communities.

The quiet, cute downtown, tucked along the waterfront, has a good collection of locally owned shops, outdoor cafes, art galleries, quaint inns, markets and New England architecture. Streets are lined with palm trees and old-fashioned street lamps. National retailers including Lowe's, Target, Walgreens and others are along U.S. Route 441 that runs through town.

Swimming, boating, fishing and golfing are all popular, and free concerts take place in Donnelly Park. Palm Island Park has one of the longest and prettiest lakeside nature walks in Florida. A stroll along the boardwalk brings a chance to glimpse blue herons, ospreys and the occasional eagle.

Festivals and events are in good supply. Each February, the town hosts the two-day juried Mount Dora Arts Festival, which draws 300,000 visitors and is considered one of the top art shows in the country. The Mount Dora Music Festival brings well known acts to town each February. October's craft fair is always well attended.

The Ice House Theatre and the Bay Street Players Community Theater add a touch of culture and have shows throughout the year.

Population: 13,500 (city proper)

Percentage of Population Age 45 or Better: 50%

Cost of Living: 2% below the national average

Median Home Price: $165,000

Median Monthly Rent: $1,400

Climate: Summer temperatures are in the 80s and 90s, and winters are mild with temperatures in the 50s, 60s and

70s. On average, the area receives 48 inches of rain each year.

At Least One Hospital Accepts Medicare Patients? No, but Florida Hospital Waterman in Tavares, about five miles away, accepts Medicare patients.

At Least One Hospital Accredited by Joint Commission? No, but Florida Hospital Waterman in Tavares, about five miles away, is accredited.

Public Transit: Yes

Crime Rate: Meets the national average

Public Library: Yes

Political Leanings: Conservative

Is Florida Considered Tax Friendly for Retirement?   Yes

Drawbacks: The tornado risk is 50% above the national average.

Notes: Mount Dora has some of the best antique shopping in the state of Florida. Renninger's Antique Center and Flea Market has hundreds of shops and booths. It is open on weekends and has a huge annual event in January.

Palm Coast, Florida

Pleasant Palm Coast sits to the west of the Intracoastal Waterway on Florida's northeastern coast. It started out in the 1960s as a planned retirement community and has been growing very fast, more than doubling in size during the last decade.

This is still primarily a residential place, but the city is developing a new, mixed use town center with parks, paths, retailers, medical offices and housing. Neighborhoods are neatly laid out, and many homes sit along a canal. Residences are mostly cookie cutter concrete block style or Mediterranean style.

The barrier island east of the Intracoastal Waterway is home to the high-end Hammock Beach Resort, which has single family homes and condominiums. Although much of the beach is privately owned by the Resort, residents enjoy a public nature preserve and several beachfront parks with boardwalks and limited water access.

Bird watching and whale spotting are popular activities, but swimming is not encouraged thanks to hidden coquina rocks and strong undercurrents. Many residents visit Flagler Beach, just 10 miles away, for water activities.

Palm Coast has a farmers' market, a Publix, a Walgreens, a Lowe's the like. A few nicer restaurants are here, but most eateries are casual.

Nightlife is quiet, but the Flagler Playhouse, a community theater, is just twelve miles away in Bunnell.

Population: 80,000 (city proper)

Percentage of Population Age 45 or Better: 57%

Cost of Living: Meets the national average

Median Home Price: $175,000

Median Rent: $1,300 per month

Climate: This area has hot, humid summers with temperatures in 80s and 90s and mild winters with temperatures in the 50s, 60s and 70s. On average, the area receives 56 inches of rain per year.

At Least One Hospital Accepts Medicare Patients? Yes

At Least One Hospital Accredited by Joint Commission? Yes

Public Transit: No, but the County provides an on demand, pre-scheduled van service.

Crime Rate: Meets the national average

Public Library: Yes

Political Leanings: Conservative

Is Florida Considered Tax Friendly for Retirement? Yes

Drawbacks: Hurricanes are a possibility, but the risk in this area is less than in more southern coastal towns. The tornado risk is 40% higher than the national average.

Notes: Palm Coast has a lot of "snowbirds."

Port Salerno, Florida

Settled in the 1920s by Italian immigrants, amiable, suburban Port Salerno sits on the St. Lucie River Inlet in southeastern Florida and straddles the Manatee Pocket, a quiet, scenic bay. Its proximity to the Atlantic Ocean has made Port Salerno an excellent base for commercial fishing, a tradition that continues today.

Port Salerno is a perfect base for recreational fisherman, too, as sea bass, grouper, kingfish, mutton snapper are particularly plentiful. The town is known for its wonderful seafood festival, which features great food, live entertainment and arts and crafts.

The Manatee Pocket waterfront boasts a cluster of ship builders, marinas, fishing charter companies and seafood restaurants. It is also home to the Fish House Art Center, a company in which artists operate galleries and studios.

The nearby St. Lucie Inlet Preserve Park, which is directly east of town, has white sand beaches that are important sea turtle nesting areas. The Anastasia Rock Reef extends along the Park's waters and is ideal for snorkeling or SCUBA diving. A boardwalk wanders from the Park's dock to the beach.

The Chapman School of Seamanship offers classes to professional and amateur mariners alike.

Home styles are mostly frame ranch rambler, concrete block ranch rambler and Florida cracker.

Population: 10,000 (city proper)

Percentage of Population Age 45 or Better: 50%

Cost of Living: 2% below the national average

Median Home Price: $165,000

Median Rent: $1,200 per month

Climate: This area has a humid subtropical climate. Summer temperatures are in the 80s and 90s, and winter temperatures are in the 60s and 70s. On average, the area receives 58 inches of rain per year.

At Least One Hospital Accepts Medicare Patients? No, but Stuart, about three miles away, has a hospital that accepts Medicare patients.

At Least One Accredited by Joint Commission? No, but Jupiter, about fifteen miles away, has a hospital that is accredited.

Public Transit: Yes, but it is limited.

Crime Rate: Below the national average

Public Library: No, but Stuart, about three miles away, has a public library.

Political Leanings: Conservative

Is Florida Considered Tax Friendly for Retirement? Yes

Drawbacks: Hurricanes and tropical storms are always a possibility.

Notes: Port Salerno is popular with "snowbirds." Most shopping and services are in nearby Stuart.

Ruskin, Florida

Unincorporated Ruskin is located in a rural part of southwestern Florida, along Tampa Bay and the Little Manatee River. It is about half way between Tampa and Bradenton and was an agricultural center for most of its 105 years. In the last decade, however, housing has sprung up, and Ruskin has nearly doubled in size. The primary draw is a mellow, "country" way of life near the water where crickets chirp and frogs sing at night.

With inlets, islets and the rarely crowded river meandering on the south side of town, Ruskin is a good spot for fishing, kayaking and canoeing. The Cockroach Aquatic Bay Preserve, 4,800 acres of protected wetlands, has recently been restored and is a particular point of pride. Two more protected natural areas are to the northeast and southeast of town.

Shellpoint Marina, situated at the mouth of the river, is not fancy but gets the job done. Ruskin's small strip of sand belongs to the very nice but private Resort and Club at Little Harbor, so beach lovers travel twenty miles south to Bradenton or six miles north to Apollo Beach.

Retailers include bait shops, thrift stores, shoe stores, discount stores and the like. Cypress Village Plaza has Home Depot, Bealls, AT&T and more. Diners, fish houses, cafes and grilles make up the dining scene.

Residents enjoy an organic market, the Ruskin Seafood and Arts Festival and the Ruskin Tomato Festival. Hillsborough Community College has classes for all ages.

Neighborhoods have everything from modest Mediterranean styles and manufactured homes to condominiums and town homes. Suburbs on the south side have homes along the shore of Little Manatee River. Sun City Center, a large 55+ community, abuts Ruskin to the east.

Population: 16,000 (city proper)

Percentage of Population Age 45 or Better: 37%

Cost of Living: 4% below the national average

Median Home Price: $165,000

Median Monthly Rent: $1,395

Climate: Summer temperatures are in the 80s and 90s with high humidity levels and frequent rainstorms. Winter temperatures are in the 60s and 70s. On average, the area receives 55 inches of rain per year.

At Least One Hospital Accepts Medicare Patients? Yes

At Least One Hospital is Accredited by the Joint Commission? Yes

Public Transit: No

Crime Rate: Meets the national average

Public Library: Yes

Political Leanings: Liberal

Is Florida Considered Tax Friendly for Retirement? Yes

Drawbacks: The poverty rate is slightly above the national average.

Notes: Ruskin tried to incorporate but failed to do so in 2007. Residents felt that the community was growing too fast without proper infrastructure and protection for the delicate marine ecosystem.

Tavares, Florida

Located in north central Florida, about thirty miles northwest of Orlando, semi-rural Tavares bills itself as

"America's Seaplane City." It borders four large lakes and has several smaller ones within town limits.

Water events and activities abound and include cypress swamp eco-cruises, a bass tournament, a race boat regatta, an antique boat show, a dragon boat show, Jet Ski races and many others. Seaplane fly-ins attract pilots from around the region and feature contests for "shortest take off," "best spot landing" and more.

The forty-slip Seaplane Base and Marina is in the simple but renovated downtown and is owned by the city. Wooten Park, along Lake Dora, has a boat dock, a popular water park and huge live oaks with dripping moss. Wooten is also the site of the Tuesday morning farmers' market.

Residents enjoy a sushi restaurant, a pizzeria, a Cajun place and a bar or two. Shopping venues are limited.

Most neighborhoods are modest with older, concrete block ranch ramblers, but there are also new subdivisions with modern home designs. Many residences, new and old, are located on a lake or in a lakeside community with water access.

Population: 15,000 (city proper)

Percentage of Population Age 45 or Better: 60%

Cost of Living: 3% below the national average

Median Home Price: $140,000

Median Monthly Rent: $1,195

Climate: Tavares has a humid subtropical climate with 48 inches of rainfall each year on average. Summer temperatures are in the 80s and 90s, and winters are mild with temperatures in the 50s, 60s and 70s.

At Least One Hospital Accepts Medicare Patients? Yes

At Least One Hospital Accredited by Joint Commission? Yes

Public Transit: Yes

Crime Rate: Below the national average

Public Library: Yes

Political Leanings: Conservative

Is Florida Considered Tax Friendly for Retirement? Yes

Drawbacks: The tornado risk is 126% higher than the national average.

Notes: Tavares is a nice town.

Winter Haven, Florida

Quiet Winter Haven is located about forty-five miles south west of Orlando in central Florida. For more than seventy years, it was home to Cypress Gardens, the popular theme park that became known as the "Water Ski Capital of the World." The park closed in 2009 and re-opened as Legoland in 2011 (with Cypress Gardens' botanic gardens still intact).

Vacationers continue to come, not just to enjoy the new theme park but to water ski on the fifty lakes in and around town. Half of these lakes are canal connected, making it easy to travel about the community via boat. Seventeen city parks are linked by the Chain of Lakes Trail, and many offer boat ramps or lake access.

Downtown has attractive one and two story buildings with cafes, shops, banks and the like. A pretty city park has a fountain and benches. Neighborhoods, some in better shape than others, are dotted with flowering dogwoods. Homes are primarily brick and concrete block ranch ramblers. There are also gated communities.

Residents enjoy a cycling classic, the Central Park Art Festival, professional golf tournaments, a Saturday Main Street Market, a Thursday farmers' market and park concerts. Theatre Winter Haven, a well-regarded community theater, mounts five main stage productions, a musical and a reading series each year.

Citi Centre Plaza has a Macy's, Belk, Lowe's, and other retailers are scattered throughout the city. Restaurants include everything from steak houses to seafood shacks with crawfish, clams and oysters.

Population: 36,000 (city proper)

Percentage of Population Age 45 or Better: 48%

Cost of Living: 7% below the national average

Median Home Price: $135,000

Median Monthly Rent: $1.150

Climate: The city has a humid, subtropical climate. Summer temperatures are in the 80s and 90s. Winter temperatures are in the 50s, 60s and 70s. On average, the area receives 51 inches of rain per year.

At Least One Hospital Accepts Medicare Patients? Yes

At Least One Accredited by Joint Commission?   Yes

Public Transit: Yes

Crime Rate: Slightly above the national average, but residents say that most crime occurs in specific areas that can be avoided.

Public Library: Yes

Political Leanings: Conservative

Is Florida Considered Tax Friendly for Retirement?   Yes

Drawbacks: The tornado risk is 147% higher than the national average.

Notes: Winter Haven has grown by 4% in the last ten years.

St. Marys, Georgia

Along the St. Marys River on Georgia's southern coast, the charming coastal village of St. Marys makes its home. The economy is tethered to tourism, commercial fishing and the U.S. military. Naval Submarine Base Kings Bay, one of only two Trident submarine bases in the world, is right next door.

Still largely undiscovered by developers, St. Marys is a closely-knit community dotted with white picket fences, quaint bed and breakfasts and live oaks draped in Spanish moss. The Historic District contains portion of the original town with 18th century commercial and residential buildings.

At the waterfront, shrimp boats are moored along the dock as they have been since the early days, and private pleasure vessels come and go in a leisurely fashion. Visitors wander in to catch the ferry to Cumberland Island National Seashore, which is just across the Cumberland Sound.

Shopping venues consist of specialty shops, boutiques and some major retailers, including Walmart, J.C. Penny and Belk. The St. Marys Community Market, an open air farmers' market, takes place every Saturday. Restaurants include some national chains, as well as locally owned cafes and diners.

Every year, Mardi Gras is celebrated with gusto, and the Rock Shrimp Festival, Hays Days and Christmas in the Park all bring out sizeable crowds. The waterfront's pretty Howard Gilman Memorial Park is a soothing spot for picnicking and watching shrimpers come in each day.

Jekyll Island and Fernandina Beach are both close by and have pretty, public beaches. Cumberland Island National Seashore has a federally-protected, unspoiled shoreline where wild hogs and feral horses roam freely. This is the place to hike, kayak, gather seashells or watch the stars.

Neighborhoods are leafy and a mixture of the modest and the extraordinary. Some have simple brick residences set on smaller lots while others contain palatial estates along the water. Osprey Cove is a beautiful 55+ development with a championship golf course and access to the Intracoastal Waterway.

Population: 18,000 (city proper)

Percentage of Population Age 45 or Better: 20%

Cost of Living: 4% below the national average

Median Home Price: $150,000

Median Monthly Rent: $1,150

Climate: Summer temperatures are in the 70s, 80s and 90s. Winter temperatures are usually in the 50s and 60s. On average, the area receives 50 inches of rain each year.

At Least One Hospital Accepts Medicare Patients? Yes

At Least One Hospital Accredited by Joint Commission? Yes

Public Transit: No

Crime Rate: Meets the national average

Public Library: Yes

Political Leanings: Conservative

Is Georgia Considered Tax Friendly for Retirement? Yes

Drawbacks: Some areas flood during intense rain storms. Road access is not as good as it could be with only three streets in and out of town. Traffic congestion builds during tourist season.

Notes: St. Marys has grown by 20% within the last decade, and it is popular with military families.

Twin Falls, Idaho

Nestled along the Snake River in rural, south central Idaho, Twin Falls is known primarily for Shoshone Falls, a nearby spectacular series of waterfalls known as the "Niagara of the West."

A relaxed place with big blue skies and little humidity, Twin Falls has a small but attractive downtown and plenty of outdoor recreation (camping, fishing, rafting and more). Neighborhoods are modest but tidy, and most homes are ranch ramblers or raised ranch ramblers.

A newer Wal-Mart, a new hospital and new housing subdivisions reflect the town's recent growth, which has been about 20% in the last decade. Residents enjoy plenty of chain restaurants and golf courses.

The College of Southern Idaho, a community college with 10,000 students, has athletic events. Its Herrett Fine Arts Center hosts college music performances. Idaho's largest planetarium is also on its campus.

Just 45 miles away, Jackpot, Nevada is home to Cactus Pete's Casino Resort.

Population: 45,000 (city proper)

Percentage of Population Age 45 or Better: 33%

Cost of Living: 4% below the national average

Median Home Price: $145,000

Median Monthly Rent: $950

Climate: This area has a semi-arid with summer temperatures in the 70s, 80s and low-90s. Winter temperatures are in the teens, 20s, 30s and 40s. The area receives little rain but about 25 inches of snow each year. The elevation is 3,600 feet above sea level.

At Least One Hospital Accepts Medicare Patients? Yes

At Least One Hospital Accredited by Joint Commission? Yes

Public Transit: The College of Southern Idaho operates Trans IV buses, a dial-a-ride service that runs Monday through Friday.

Crime Rate: Meets the national average

Public Library: Yes

Political Leanings: Very conservative

Is Idaho Considered Tax Friendly for Retirement? Yes

Drawbacks: Wind is common, and Twin Falls does not have a lot a lot in the way of cultural amenities.

Notes: Shoshone Falls is taller than Niagara Falls. The Twin Falls Public Library receives very good reviews. Twin Falls sits in the middle of an agricultural region. The city has a sizeable Mormon population.

Slidell, Louisiana

Sleepy Slidell sits along the northeastern shores of 630-acre Lake Pontchartrain in southeastern Louisiana. It is just 25 miles from New Orleans via a 24 mile long causeway across the lake. Hit hard by Hurricane Katrina in 2005, Slidell suffered storm surges up to fifteen feet in some areas. The city has since recovered.

Southern hospitality is the hallmark of this quiet town. It has a cute, ten square block historic downtown and some beautiful old homes, many built during the Victorian era when well-to-do New Orleanians headed to the "Northshore" for summer relaxation. Cultural amenities are not in great supply, but boating and fishing keep many a resident busy.

Annual festivals include the Bayou Jam Concert, the Art League's Artist of the Year Exhibit, the Fall Street Fair, the Arts Evening Festival and Christmas Under the Stars. Scenic bayous abound, and with New Orleans so close, fun French Quarter strolling, professional football games and dining in eclectic restaurants are close at hand. The Gulf itself is just a 45 minute drive away.

City parks keep Slidell looking green, and three golf courses, Oak Harbor, Pinewood and Royal, give duffers and low handicappers plenty of places to play. Tammany Trace is a 31 mile long paved trail and equestrian path. It runs not only through Slidell but through four other towns and overlooks bayous and streams.

Two wildlife preserves, the Bogue Chitto National Wildlife Refuge and the Bayou Sauvage National Wildlife Refuge, are home to endangered species, including the ringedsawback turtle, the American alligator and the gopher tortoise.

Population: 28,000 (city proper)

Percentage of Population Age 45 or Better: 38%

Cost of Living: 5% below the national average

Median Home Price: $140,000

Median Monthly Rent: $1,125

Climate: This area has a humid subtropical climate with summer temperatures in the 80s and 90s. Winters are generally mild with winter temperatures in the 40s and 50s. On average, the area receives 62 inches of rain each year.

At Least One Hospital Accepts Medicare Patients? Yes

At Least One Hospital Accredited by Joint Commission? Yes

Public Transit: The County provides a curb to curb, on demand van service.

Crime Rate: Meets the national average

Public Library: Yes

Political Leanings: Conservative

Is Louisiana Considered Tax Friendly for Retirement? Yes

Drawbacks: Hurricanes and the flooding that comes with them are always a threat, especially south of Interstate 12. The tornado risk is 120% higher than the national average.

Notes: The St. Tammany Parish has a branch library that offers a library loan program, public computers with Internet access, computer classes, tax assistance and even books.

Canadian Lakes, Michigan

Pretty Canadian Lakes is a year-round resort community, property owners' association and census designated place located in central Michigan. It started out in the mid-1960s and is today particularly popular with empty nesters and retirees.

The resort sits amid rolling hills and Amish farms and is known for its abundant outdoor recreation. It sprawls across 7,000 acres, 2,000 acres of which are open space dotted with lakes, ponds, pools, parks, golf courses and beaches. A castle, a private plane landing strip, a restaurant, a fitness center, clubhouses and sixty social clubs are here, too

Some of the resort's 11 lakes are all-sport and some are no-wake, and a fishery supplies the lakes with bass and blue gill. The community sponsors a concert series as well as golf events and fishing tournaments.

The Little Muskegon River runs through Canadian Lakes and is a popular place for canoeing and fishing. The nearby Manistee National Forest offers biking, camping, hunting, and hiking.

Homes, many nestled in the woods or along the water, are mostly A-frames and ranch ramblers.

Population: 3,000 (city proper)

Percentage of Population Age 45 or Better: 73%

Cost of Living: Meets the national average

Median Home Price: $195,000

Median Monthly Rent: $950

Climate: Summer temperatures are in the 70s and 80s. Winter temperatures are in the teens and 20s. On average, the area receives 55 inches of snow and 32 inches of rain each year.

At Least One Hospital Accepts Medicare Patients? No, but the one in Stanwood, about twelve miles away, accepts Medicare patients.

At Least One Hospital Accredited by Joint Commission? No, but Big Rapids, about twelve miles away, has a hospital that is accredited.

Public Transit: No

Crime Rate: Well below the national average

Public Library: Yes, a small lending library

Political Leanings: Conservative

Is Michigan Considered Tax Friendly for Retirement? Somewhat

Drawbacks: The town is isolated.

Notes: Canadian Lakes has grown by 25% within the last decade and still has a large number of undeveloped home sites. The air quality is outstanding.

Ocean Springs, Mississippi

On Mississippi's eastern Gulf Coast, the quiet hamlet of Ocean Springs sits on Biloxi Bay and has a long history. It began as the first permanent settlement in French Louisiana in 1699. In the mid-19th century, it became a resort town and garnered accolades for its healing waters. In 2005, it was severely damaged by Hurricane Katrina and even today continues to rebuild.

Fishing is a way of life in Ocean Springs and always has been. Each morning fishing boats set out to sea, returning in the afternoon with nets full of fresh crab, shrimp and oysters. Much of this bounty finds its way into dozens of locally owned markets and very good restaurants.

In recent years, Ocean Springs has also become known for its eclectic arts scene. The Walter Anderson Museum of Art celebrates the work of its namesake, and the beautiful Mary C. O'Keefe Cultural Center has art classes, exhibits and performances. The Art and Antiques Market, open just six times per year, showcases handcrafts, antiques and collectibles.

The downtown is cute and leafy with galleries, pubs, sidewalk cafes and shops. Residents enjoy a Saturday farmers' market, an organic grocery, three golf courses, many festivals and plenty of opportunities for swimming and boating. Front Beach and East Beach have both been restored since Katrina and have a boardwalk.

Housing stock includes ranch ramblers, plantations, Colonials and stilt homes. Neighborhoods are generally well kept.

Population: 18,000 (city proper)

Percentage of Population Age 45 or Better: 37%

Cost of Living: 5% below the national average

Median Home Price: $140,000

Median Monthly Rent: $1,100

Climate: Ocean Springs is hot and sticky in the summer and mild and a little less sticky in the winter. Summer temperatures are in the 80s and 90s, and winter temperatures are the 50s and 60s. On average, the area receives 62 inches of rain per year.

At Least One Hospital Accepts Medicare Patients? Yes

At Least One Hospital Accredited by Joint Commission? Yes

Public Transit: Yes, provided by CTA. It makes stop at Walmart, the hospital, the post office and a nearby casino.

Crime Rate: Below the national average

Public Library: Yes

Political Leanings: Very conservative

Is Mississippi Considered Tax Friendly for Retirement? Yes

Drawbacks: The tornado risk is 85% greater than the national average. Homeowner insurance is expensive. Traffic throughout the city and along the main highway is frequently congested.

Notes: Some people say that the city is cliquish and a place where everyone knows everyone else's business.

The median household income is above the national median.

Saranac Lake, New York

In northern New York, the picturesque village of Saranac Lake is in a region called Tri-Lakes and is tucked within scenic Adirondack Park, the largest forest preserve in the U.S. Partially situated along the pretty shores of Lake Flower, the village started out as a logging settlement and later gained fame as a vacation playground for the nation's elite, including Al Jolson, Albert Einstein and Mark Twain.

Saranac Lake is recognized for its historic structures, 186 of which are listed on the National Register of Historic Places, and for its surrounding tableau of forests, hills, rivers and lakes. The town has an easy pace, a friendly reputation and has been hailed as one of the best small towns in America by several national publications.

Five named lakes are within a five minute drive, and Lake Placid's 2,200 acres of smooth water are just seven miles away. During the summer, hiking, canoeing, golfing and camping are popular, and in the winter, cross country skiing, snow shoeing and down hill skiing at Mt. Pisgah Ski Area are the activities of choice.

Residents also enjoy a two week winter carnival with a king and a queen, a parade and a colorfully-lit ice palace made with ice carved from Lake Flower.

Six art galleries, a year-round professional theatre, live concerts and art festivals contribute to the town's healthy arts scene. A Third Thursday Artwalk is a great way to see local artists' works. During the last weekend of every

September, more than thirty area artists open their homes and studios for the annual Artists at Work Studio Tour.

Home styles include cabin, clapboard saltbox, contemporary, ranch rambler, bungalow and more. Many residences are nestled in the woods.

Population: 5,500 (city proper)

Percentage of Population Age 45 or Better: 38%

Cost of Living: Meets the national average

Median Home Price: $175,000

Median Monthly Rent: $1,500 (rent prices are difficult to pin down because many homes are vacation rentals)

Climate: June, July and August temperatures are in the 60s and 70s, and winter temperatures are in the teens and 20s. On average, the area receives 120 inches of snow and 40 inches of rain each year.

At Least One Hospital Accepts Medicare Patients? Yes

At Least One Hospital Accredited by Joint Commission? Yes

Public Transit: Yes

Crime Rate: Below the national average

Public Library Yes

Political Leanings: Liberal

Is New York Considered Tax Friendly for Retirement? No

Drawbacks: Black flies can be a nuisance in the summer.

Notes: Winters are long. North Country Community College has classes for all ages.

Lake Waccamaw, North Carolina

In southeastern North Carolina, the quiet little town of Lake Waccamaw is on the northern edge of oval-shaped, 9,000-acre Lake Waccamaw.   Swampland and state park land surround the rest of the lake's 14 mile shoreline.

Large residences, many of which are second homes or vacation homes, sit along the water and have a private pier or boat dock.   Inland homes, which are generally more modest, year-round residences, sit on wooded lots in low density neighborhoods.

The lake itself is tea-colored and only seven and a half feet deep. It is part of Lake Waccamaw State Park and teems with fish, some of which are found nowhere else on earth. The North Carolina Division of Parks also stocks the lake with bluegill, largemouth bass, shellcracker and more.   Ski boats, fishing boats and sailboats dot the water in season, and hikers enjoy a number of all weather trails that meander through the Park.

The town has a small strip mall, a museum, a bank, churches, a pharmacy, a fishing supply store and some restaurants, including Dale's Seafood Restaurant. It has its own dock, serves Calabash-style food, which is breaded and deep fried, and is known for its oyster roast.

Population: 1,500 (city proper)

Percentage of Population Age 45 or Better: 54%

Cost of Living: Meets the national average

Median Home Price: $195,000

Median Monthly Rent: $1,595

Climate: Summer temperatures are in the 80s and 90s, and winters are mild with temperatures in 40s, 50s and 60s. On average, the area receives 53 inches of rain per year.

At Least One Hospital Accepts Medicare Patients?   No

At Least One Hospital Accredited by Joint Commission? No. Whiteville, nine miles away, has a hospital, but it is not accredited. The nearest accredited hospital, which accepts Medicare patients, is in Elizabethtown, about 20 miles away.

Public Transit: No

Crime Rate: Below the national average

Public Library: Yes

Political Leanings: Conservative

Is North Carolina Considered Tax Friendly for Retirement? Somewhat

Drawbacks: The poverty rate is above the national level.

Notes: Although it does not have a hospital, Lake Waccamaw has a small medical clinic.

Swansboro, North Carolina

Founded in 1783 and nestled between the Intracoastal Waterway and the White Oak River on North Carolina's mid-coast, homey Swansboro got its start as a shipbuilding center. It is a laid back, friendly place and in no hurry to become a tourist destination.

Swansboro is on the southern end of an oceanfront stretch known as the Crystal Coast. By land, North Carolina Highway 24 (NC-24) is the only way in and out of town, and vacationers often pass through on their way to Emerald Isle, a beach community to the east. The fact that Swansboro is paid little attention by tourists has helped it retain its mellow charm and rich quality of life.

An estuary brimming with dolphins, herons and ospreys is just beyond the waterfront. Boats of all shapes and sizes bob in the water, and gentle waves lap at the docks. The sea air soothes, and the relaxed, authentic coastal ambiance entices. Before long, the spell is cast, and nearly all who enter Swansboro feel right at home.

Seventy-four of Swansboro's buildings are on the National Register of Historic Places, and architectural styles include Federal, Craftsman and Greek Revival. The historic downtown is cute and has kept the flavor of an earlier, seafaring time. The main street, Front Street, is lined with various shops and boutiques, including Russell's Old Tyme Shoppe, a fun gift and home-furnishings store.

There are enough service providers such as dentists, veterinarians and handymen to meet most needs, but national retailers, including Lowe's, Walgreens and Walmart, are also close at hand.

Residents also enjoy a good selection of delicious restaurants, including Captain Charlie's Seafood Paradise, which serves what may be the world's finest fried seafood. For fresh, healthy food, the downtown farmers' market is open Wednesdays and Saturdays from May through October.

With three marinas, Swansboro sees plenty of boat traffic, some local and some transient. Casper's, in the center of the waterfront, is the primary marina. Flying Bridge Marina is mostly composed of "boataminiums" (boat condos). Bogue Inlet offers quick ocean access for deep sea fishing and SCUBA diving.

There are dozens of public beach access points in and around town, and the beaches are clean and often uncrowded. Nearby Hammocks Beach State Park is a nearly 900-acre recreation area that is a nationally recognized coastal wildlife nature preserve and nesting area for loggerhead sea turtles. Two islands make up the Park, and access to Bear Island is by ferry only but is worth the 15 minute trip. It is an excellent spot for kayaking.

Housing stock ranges from early-20th century cottages to new construction. Most upscale neighborhoods and subdivisions have private community boat slips

Population: 2,800 (city proper)

Percentage of Population Age 45 or Better: 40%

Cost of Living: Meets the national average

Median Home Price: $170,000

Median Monthly Rent: $1,425

Climate: The climate is sub-topical. Summer temperatures are in the 80s and 90s, and winter temperatures are in the 30s, 40s and 50s. The average annual rainfall is 57 inches.

At Least One Hospital Accepts Medicare Patients? No, but Carteret General Hospital is in Morehead City, just two miles away, and it accepts Medicare patients.

At Least One Hospital Accredited by Joint Commission? No, but Carteret General Hospital is in Morehead City, just two miles away, and it is accredited.

Public Transit: No

Crime Rate: Meets the national average

Public Library: Yes. The Onslow County Public Library is small but has two dozen public computers with internet access

Political Leanings: Conservative

Is North Carolina Considered Tax Friendly for Retirement? Somewhat

Drawbacks: Sewers have been known to back up during heavy rains. The town is completely exposed if a hurricane should strike.

Notes: Swansboro has grown by 30% in the last decade, and long-time locals worry about their community losing its quaint seaside charm.

Irmo, South Carolina

Irmo is in the heart of South Carolina's Midlands, just outside of the capital city of Columbia and almost halfway between the state's mountains and its beaches. It has a small town charm and a good reputation.

The town is a gateway to 50,000-acre Lake Murray, a reservoir fed by the Saluda River, and sits along its shore. With more than 500 miles of shoreline, the lake is a magnet for water devotees from around the region. It has marinas, recreation areas, and the Billy Dreher Island State Park. Boating, water skiing and fishing, particularly for shellcrackers and large mouth bass, are popular.

Saluda Shoals Park has kayak rentals and guided horseback rides. The miles of trails in the adjacent Harbison State Forest meander through verdant hardwood forests and cross streams and glades.

Irmo's Okra Strut is a long standing tradition that celebrates small town life. It features live music, a parade, street dancing and plenty of food. The community orchestra has a Sunday concert series. Ten golf courses are within easy reach.

Home styles include brick ranch rambler, plantation, Craftsman and more in nicely maintained neighborhoods.

Population: 12,000 (city proper)

Percentage of Population Age 45 or Better: 27%

Cost of Living: 2% below the national average

Median Home Price: $160,000

Median Monthly Rent: $1,150

Climate: Summer temperatures are in the 80s and 90s, and winter temperatures are in the 30s, 40s and 50s. On average, the area receives 50 inches of rain per year.

At Least One Hospital Accepts Medicare Patients? No, but Columbia has a hospital that accepts Medicare patients.

At Least One Hospital Accredited by Joint Commission? No, but Columbia has a hospital that is accredited.

Public Transit: No

Crime Rate: Meets the national average

Public Library: The northern branch of the Columbia library system serves as the Irmo library.

Political Leanings: Liberal

Is South Carolina Considered Tax Friendly for Retirement? Yes

Drawbacks: None

Notes: Irmo has grown by 7% in the last decade.

Little River, South Carolina

Along South Carolina's Grand Strand, the state's famous 60 mile long stretch of beach and entertainment venues, the gentle Intracoastal Waterway community of Little River makes its home. Once a pirate lair and always a commercial fishing and shrimping village, the town is known for its authentic coastal ambiance and delicious seafood.

Residents enjoy eight golf courses and three marinas. Two large floating casinos are moored at the dock and draw locals and vacationers alike. Vereen Memorial Historical Gardens, with its marshes, small islands, pathways, boardwalks and gazebo, is a soothing place to spend an afternoon. La Belle Amie Vineyard is open to the public with a wine tasting room and live music events.

Each year, Little River plays host to a number of fun festivals. The Blue Crab Festival, Oktoberfest, the Intracoastal Waterway Boat Parade, the Shrimp and Jazz Festival and the Christmas Market are just a few.

Fresh seafood catches arrive each afternoon and are served in the numerous waterfront restaurants. Shopping venues are primarily locally owned shops and boutiques. Major retailers are found in North Myrtle Beach, about eight miles to the south.

Homes include simple bungalows, brick contemporaries, ranch ramblers and some spectacular mansions. Condos and town homes are in good supply as well.

Population: 11,000 (city proper)

Percentage of Population Age 45 or Better: 55%

Cost of Living: 2% below the national average

Median Home Price: $155,000

Median Monthly Rent: $1,250

Climate: Summers are hot and humid with temperatures in the 80s and 90s. Winters are mild with temperatures in the 40s, 50s and 60s. On average, the area receives 52 inches of rain per year.

At Least One Hospital Accepts Medicare Patients? No, but Grand Strand Regional Medical Center, fifteen miles away in Myrtle Beach, accepts Medicare patients.

At Least One Hospital Accredited by Joint Commission? No, but Grand Strand Regional Medical Center, fifteen miles away in Myrtle Beach, is accredited.

Public Transit: Coast Transit Plus provides on demand van service.

Crime Rate: Below the national average

Public Library: Yes

Political Leanings: Conservative

Is South Carolina Considered Tax Friendly for Retirement? Yes

Drawbacks: Hurricanes and tropical storms are not unknown here.

Notes: Residents enjoy easy access to the Grand Stand and several highways. The beach is about ten minutes away. Little River is growing, increasing its population by nearly 50% within the last decade.

Northlake, South Carolina

Northlake is a residential community situated in upstate South Carolina, about thirty miles southwest of Greenville. It has grown by nearly 25% in the last decade, and much of this growth is due to Northlake's waterfront location and reasonable cost of living.

The town sits on both sides of a northern offshoot of 56,000-acre Lake Hartwell, a man-made reservoir that is one of the most popular recreation areas in the South. Water skiing, fishing, camping, swimming and wildlife watching are popular activities with tourists and locals alike.

Northlake neighborhoods are leafy, meandering, low density and well-tended with new Craftsman styles, plantation styles and brick ranch ramblers. Homes directly on the water tend to be large and have covered boat docks.

Nearly all shopping and dining options are in Anderson, population 26,000 and the County seat, about five miles away.

Population: 4,250 (city proper)

Percentage of Population Age 45 or Better: 43%

Cost of Living: Meets the national average

Median Home Price: $175,000

Median Monthly Rent: $1,125

Climate: Summer temperatures are in the 80s and 90s. Winter temperatures are in 30s, 40s and 50s. On average, the area receives 50 inches of rain each year.

At Least One Hospital Accepts Medicare Patients? No, but Anmed Health in Anderson, five miles away, accepts Medicare patients.

At Least One Hospital Accredited by Joint Commission? No, but Anmed Health in Anderson, five miles away, is accredited.

Public Transit: No

Crime Rate: Below the national average

Public Library: No

Political Leanings: Very conservative

Is South Carolina Considered Tax Friendly for Retirement?
Yes

Drawbacks: The tornado risk is 70% higher than the
national average, and the air quality is below the national
average.

Notes: None

Port Royal, South Carolina

Sleepy Port Royal sits along Port Royal Sound on the
South Carolina coast and is just across the water from
8,100-acre Marine Corps Recruit Depot Parris Island
(which is actually part of the city).   Visited by the Spanish
in the early-16th century, the flags of six governments,
Spain, France, England, Scotland, the United States and the
Confederate States of America, have flown over Port
Royal.

With the town situated between the Beaufort River and
Battery Creek, boating and fishing are way of life here.
Quiet waterways twist past cypress swamps, historic
plantation homes, tidal marshes and estuaries.

The Old Village, along Paris Avenue, has shops,
restaurants, a farmers' market, a StreetMusic on Paris
Avenue concert series, an annual oyster roast, the popular
Soft Shell Crab Fest and various restaurants (11th Street

Dockside in particular gets rave reviews). This section of town also includes the iconic, working shrimp docks.

The city has recently undertaken some large projects, including making the Cypress Wetlands more accessible. A bird sanctuary for brown pelicans, peregrine falcons and bald eagles is also planned. The Sands municipal beach has picnic areas, a boat ramp and a boardwalk. Miles of nature trails wind in and around the area.

Port Royal boasts of its "new urbanism" and has some appealing, high density homes with a very European feel, as well as cute bungalows, antebellum style homes and contemporary design residences. The Shed hosts concerts and plays, and thirteen golf courses are within a 10 mile drive.

Population: 12,000 (city proper)

Percentage of Population Age 45 or Better: 28%

Cost of Living: 5% below the national average

Median Home Price: $135,000

Median Monthly Rent: $950

Climate: The area has a subtropical climate. Summers temperatures in the 80s and 90s, and winters are mild with temperatures in the 40s, 50s, and 60s. On average, the area receives 48 inches of rain per year.

At Least One Hospital Accepts Medicare Patients? No, but Beaufort Memorial Hospital, just a couple of miles north, accepts Medicare patients.

At Least One Accredited by Joint Commission? No, but Beaufort Memorial Hospital, just a couple of miles north, is accredited.

Public Transit: The County has a van program that provides transportation to social events, medical and recreational activities.

Crime Rate: Below the national average

Public Library: No

Political Leanings: Conservative

Is South Carolina Considered Tax Friendly for Retirement? Yes

Drawbacks: The dock situation has been causing some economic issues, although the city says its finances are sound.

Notes: The city blends into Beaufort to the north, and it has a naval hospital. Parris Island trains 17,000 marines each year. Retirees enjoy the area because it is close to Hilton Head Island.

Norris, Tennessee

Tucked away in the rolling hills of rural northeastern Tennessee, Norris is situated along the shores of 34,000-acre Norris Lake.

The town started out in 1933 as a planned community built by the Tennessee Valley Authority (TVA) and was originally designed to demonstrate the benefits of cooperative living. As a result, Norris is today listed on the National Register of Historic Places.

TVA town planners based their design on the English garden design movement of the late-19th century. The town was laid out to be entirely walkable, and homes were built at angles to one another. Norris was also the first community in the country to employ greenbelts as a design feature.

Residents cherish Norris' Norman Rockwell-like quality, with its cute homes and New England-style town square that has a post office, a family owned grocery store, a real estate office, a diner, a gas station and the library. There are also a couple of parks and six churches.

Evening concerts, a farmers' market and festivals in the square help create a sense of community. So does the walking trail that winds its way past every residence.

The lake provides a wonderful backdrop, and recreation areas along the water are the place for hiking, picnicking and just enjoying some solitude. Boating and fishing for rockfish, walleye and bass are always popular.

Housing stock includes ranch ramblers, cottages, salt boxes and more. Some homes are relatively new, but many of them are the original TVA structures.

Population: 1,800 (city proper)

Percentage of Population Age 45 or Better: 48%

Cost of Living: Meets the national average

Median Home Price: $175,000

Median Monthly Rent: $1,300

Climate: On average, the area receives 55 inches of rain and an occasional dusting of snow each year. Summer temperatures are in the 80s and 90s, and winter temperatures are in the 30s, 40s and 50s.

At Least One Hospital Accepts Medicare Patients? No, but one that does is just twelve miles away in Oak Ridge.

At Least One Accredited by Joint Commission? No, but Oak Ridge, twelve miles away, has an accredited hospital.

Public Transit: No

Crime Rate: Well below the national average

Public Library: Yes

Political Leanings: Very conservative

Is Tennessee Considered Tax Friendly for Retirement?
Yes

Drawbacks: None

Notes: Vacation home owners have discovered Norris in recent years.

Marble Falls, Texas

Built along the banks of Texas' Colorado River, comfortable Marble Falls is in the middle of the Texas Hill Country and the Highland Lakes Chain. It was founded by a Confederate general in the late-19th century and has mushroomed by nearly 20% in the last ten years.

The falls from which the town takes its name were submerged under a dam in the 1940s. Today, the resulting

19,000-acre Lake Travis is home to Lakefest, one of the largest drag boat races in the United States. Marble Falls is also bracketed by Lake LBJ and Lake Travis, both of which are popular with fishermen and campers.

The slightly rustic Main Street District has wide streets, galleries, sculptures, a cinema and restaurants. There is at least one health food store, and national retailers include Walmart, Walgreens and Bealls.

Two local wineries have tours and tastings, and Hidden Falls Golf Club has eighteen holes. Marble Falls manages several of its own parks, with many of the town's events held at Johnson Park.

The Highland Arts Guild and Gallery offers classes and workshops, and the nearby Hill Country Community Theatre has been producing plays since 1991. Residents also enjoy a plein air competition and a "starving artist" show,

Homes sit in tidy neighborhoods laid out along grids. Brick ranch ramblers, country bungalows and horse properties are common.

Population: 6,500 (city proper)

Percentage of Population Age 45 or Better: 30%

Cost of Living: 2% below the national average

Median Home Price: $165,000

Median Monthly Rent: $1,245

Climate: Summer temperatures are in the 80s, 90s and even low-100s. Winter temperatures are in the 30s, 40s and

50s. On average, the area receives 30 inches of rain per year.

At Least One Hospital Accepts Medicare Patients? No, but Seton Highlands Lakes is twelve miles away and accepts Medicare patients.

At Least One Hospital Accredited by Joint Commission? No, but Seton Highlands Lakes is twelve miles away and is accredited.

Public Transit: No

Crime Rate: Below the national average

Public Library: Yes

Political Leanings: Very, very conservative

Is Texas Considered Tax Friendly for Retirement? Yes

Drawbacks: The tornado risk is 78% higher than the national average.

Notes: The water levels in the lakes around Marble Falls are said to be some of the highest in the area.

Port Angeles, Washington

Sturdy, working class Port Angeles is a harbor town that sits on the northern shores of the stunning Olympic Peninsula in northwestern Washington. It was built on the site of two Indian villages, and the Ediz Hook, a sandspit that extends into the Strait of Juan de Fuca, helped create its deep water port. For many years Port Angeles was a mill town, producing lumber, pulp and paper.

As the headquarters of the Olympic National Park, today the town's economy is mostly dependent on tourism. The park has an amazing variety of ecosystems within its boundaries, everything from ancient glaciers to temperate rainforest, and it attracts all sorts of outdoor adventurers.

Lake Crescent and Hurricane Ridge are two popular park destinations. Closer in, the Olympic Discovery Trail is a greenway that circumnavigates Port Angeles and Sequim. The town itself manages numerous parks, a stadium, a pool, and a community center.

The downtown is authentic with a touristy bent. Buildings are red brick and house cafes, bookstores and antique shops.

Peninsula College, a community college with 10,000 part-time students, is based in the town, as is Clallam County's historical society and museum.

The Port Angeles Symphony conducts a busy season of pops and chamber concerts, and the Port Angeles Community Theater has been producing plays for more than 50 years. Several highly-rated wineries dot the area.

Home styles are eclectic, including Cape Cods, bungalows, Craftsman, raised ranch and more. Most residences sit on lush lots.

Population: 19,500 (city proper)

Percentage of Population Age 45 or Better: 44%

Cost of Living: Meets the national average

Median Home Price: $175,000

Median Monthly Rent: $1,185

Climate: Port Angeles sits in the rain shadow of the Olympic Mountains and receives about 25 inches of rain and a dusting of snow each year. Summer temperatures are in the 50s, 60s and 70s, and winter temperatures are in the 30s and 40s.

At Least One Hospital Accepts Medicare Patients? Yes

At Least One Hospital Accredited by Joint Commission? Yes

Public Transit: Yes, and Port Angeles is served by an international ferry and airport.

Crime Rate: Meets the national average

Public Library: Yes

Political Leanings: Nearly split down the middle

Is Washington Considered Tax Friendly for Retirement? Yes

Drawbacks: The crime rate meets the national average but has been slightly higher than that in years past.

Notes: Shopping and services are adequate, but many residents travel to Sequim, 30 miles away, for supplies.

Thanks for reading!

About the Author

Kris Kelley lives in beautiful Colorado has been finding and reviewing great places to retire since 2006. She is an avid traveler, always looking for that hidden gem of a town, whether it be along an ocean, in a desert or on a mountaintop.

More Titles by the Author

Made in the USA
San Bernardino, CA
12 December 2017